In this series –

RUMI READINGS
FOR
SELF-ESTEEM

RUMI READINGS
FOR
SELF-ESTEEM

JALALUDDIN RUMI

The Scheherazade Foundation

The Scheherazade Foundation CIC
85 Great Portland Street
London
W1W 7LT
United Kingdom
www.SF.Charity
info@SF.Charity

First published by The Scheherazade Foundation CIC, 2025

RUMI READINGS FOR SELF-ESTEEM

© The Scheherazade Foundation

The Scheherazade Foundation asserts the right to be identified as the Author
of the Work in accordance with the Copyright, Designs and Patents Act 1988.

A CIP catalogue record for this title is available from the British Library.

ISBN 978-1-915311-79-5

Introduction

Jalaluddin Rumi was born in Balkh, Afghanistan, in the year 1207, and died in Konya, Turkey, in 1273.

During the sixty-six years spanning this pair of dates, he produced a range of extraordinary work in Persian which, today, is classed as 'Sufi Mysticism'.

In the seven and a half centuries since his death, Rumi's corpus, which includes *The Masnavi* and *Fihi Ma Fihi*, has been circulated widely across the Near East, the Arab world, and Central Asia.

Generations of students continue to commit selections of the 60,000 verses to heart, and allow Rumi's way of thought to permeate through all areas of their lives.

Although Orientalists venturing eastward from Europe in the 1700s occasionally made note of Sufi Mysticism, they tended to witness it through the more theatrical frills – such as 'whirling dervishes' – rather than through a deep appreciation of the texts.

It wasn't until the close of the nineteenth century that the first wholescale translations of Rumi's written work began to appear in Europe.

Even then, they remained very much the purview of a few academics, whose translations were – even for the time – laden with indescribably floral and cumbersome prose.

Although in the Occident, students would find themselves scrutinizing Rumi's corpus, it wasn't until more recently that accessible appreciations of his work became available.

A few years before his death, I asked my father – the Sufi scholar and thinker Idries Shah – for his thoughts on Rumi's legacy in the West.

Sitting in his favourite chair, a porcelain cup of green tea in hand, he looked at me hard.

'I never cease to be amazed,' he said.

'Amazed by what?'

'By the way people don't take what's perfectly packaged, and ready and waiting for them, but rather obsess with something else.'

'With what?'

'With endless and nonsensical trimmings, trappings, and paraphernalia.'

My father sipped his tea.

After a moment of silent thought, he continued:

'Read Rumi in the original Persian,' he said, 'and so delicate are the verses that you have tears rolling down your cheeks. Yet here in the West, it's served up as something submerged in a thick, glutinous gravy, so much so that its utterly inedible.'

I reminded my father that a series of publications had recently found their way to press – publications that presented Rumi's couplets in an utterly new way.

Stripped bare of what my father had referred to as 'gravy', they were light.

Indeed, they were lighter than light.

My father rolled his eyes at the thought.

'In any other place, and at any other time,' he said, 'people would be up in arms. Or, if they weren't, they'd be laughing until their sides split. Imagine it – Western poets with absolutely no knowledge of the original Persian text touting new, bestselling editions of Rumi's work! It's what we call "The Soup of the Soup of the Soup".'

In the years since my father's death, Occidental society has been flooded with all things Rumi.

Couplets ascribed to him are read solemnly at weddings across the United States, Europe, and beyond.

Wisdom drawn from his poetry is tattooed daily over the backs and limbs of Hollywood A-listers.

But the precious words uttered at weddings, tattooed into skin, and quoted in abundance, hold little or no bearing to the original verses of Jalaluddin Rumi.

So, there it is…

The great Sufi Master's wisdom available:

(a) in a form that's unreadable because it's all covered in glutinous gravy, or

(b) in another form that's completely distorted – the Soup of the Soup of the Soup.

One thing that *is* evident is that the West can benefit enormously from a clean, clear rendition of Rumi's thinking – as the East has done over the last seven hundred years.

For this reason, we have commissioned entirely new translations, gleaned in particular from *The Masnavi*. Selected and translated by native Persian-speaking scholars, the emphasis has been on maintaining the lightness of Rumi's poetry.

In an age of relentless speed and digital overload, and so as to allow the work to be accessed by those who may benefit from it most, we have arranged a series of bite-sized morsels by way of theme.

We encourage you to do what students, scholars, and ordinary people have done across the East for centuries...

To pick a single couplet, or a handful – and to read them over and over, allowing them to seed themselves in your mind.

Little by little, having taken root, they will blossom and bear fruit.

Tahir Shah

How to Use This Book

Rumi Readings for Self-Esteem

This book is an invitation to remember who you are.

Not the version others expect, or the one you perform – but the self that quietly waits beneath the noise.

The one that knows its own worth.

The one that has not forgotten how to shine.

Rumi Readings for Self-Esteem brings together one hundred selections from the original Persian works of Jalaluddin Rumi, translated freshly and faithfully by The Scheherazade Foundation. These verses are not sentimental affirmations. They are **truths** – grounded in centuries of spiritual insight and human experience.

Self-esteem, for Rumi, is not about pride or surface confidence.

It is about **knowing your origin**.

It is about aligning with the deeper self – the one made of light, resilience, dignity, and love.

It is about seeing clearly, acting truthfully, and remembering that your value does not come from comparison, but from essence.

Let this book accompany you as you return to that essence – gently, honestly, and in your own time.

Read It Like a Mirror

Each quote in this book is a mirror.

It reflects a part of you – sometimes one you forgot, sometimes one you've been avoiding.

It may show your strength. It may show your fear. It may offer a quiet reminder: *You are more than you believe.*

These quotes are arranged in ten parts – from traits of self-esteem and ways to grow it, to the problems that arise when it's lacking, and the deeper forces that either hinder or help us see our true worth.

You can move through them in order, or open the book at random. Either way, let each quote meet you where you are.

Go Slowly

There is no need to rush.

This book is not meant to be consumed – it is meant to be **lived with**.

Try reading one quote a day. Or one each week.

Let it sit with you as you go about your day.

Return to it when the inner voice becomes unkind. Let the words interrupt the doubt.

You don't need to understand everything. Some lines will land. Others will unfold slowly.

This is part of the process.

Listen to What It Stirs

After reading a quote, ask:

- What part of me does this speak to?
- Where have I lost sight of myself?
- What is this reminding me to reclaim?

Let these questions guide your attention inward – not to judge, but to listen.

If you feel drawn to write, reflect, or respond in a deeper way, you can try keeping a journal. Ask questions. Let it prompt memories. Or just write what you're feeling, even if it has nothing to do with the quote.

Let it be a tool – not a task.

For Those Rebuilding

This book is especially for those who feel fractured.

For those recovering from criticism, heartbreak, injustice, invisibility.

For those learning how to stand tall again – or for the first time.

Rumi's voice does not rush you.

He knew the soul unfolds slowly.

He knew how long it can take to believe you're enough.

He reminds us that the deepest self-worth does not come from achievement – but from presence. From integrity. From truth.

Let that be enough for now.

A Voice to Keep Close

You may want to carry this book with you – to read in quiet moments, between classes, before a conversation, after a hard day.

Let it be a pocket of clarity in a noisy world.

You may also want to share it – with a friend, a mentor, a student, a child. One quote can become a lifeline. One truth, remembered, can shift an entire way of seeing.

The Return

Self-esteem is not built once.

It is returned to again and again.

This book will not 'fix' you – because you are not broken.

It will not make you someone new – because the real work is remembering who you've always been.

Rumi writes in this volume:

'You may understand the value of every commodity. But if you are oblivious to your own worth, you are a fool.'

So come back to your worth.

Come back to your dignity.
Come back to the voice inside you that knows.

This book is only a guide.
The journey – beautifully, courageously – is yours.

Part 1

The Trait
of Self-Esteem

1

You are not merely an individual, dear friend;
you embody the universe and a vast, deep ocean.

2

The devil is inherently blind and deaf;
how could a cow recognize a jewel in the mud?

3

The essence and nature of the soul are revelatory: greater awareness correlates with a more vibrant life.

4

Look within and abandon fruitless searching;
search inside yourself rather than
constantly seeking validation from others.

5

The divine spirit proclaims:
'Do not despair,'
like a father searching for his lost son,
looking in every corner.

6

A hidden treasure was revealed by the Creator, raising earthly beings above the celestial realms.

7

A king's falcon would think it beneath itself
to hunt a mere partridge.

8

How can a stone show lush green growth in spring?
Be like the soil, and vibrant blooms
will burst forth from you.

9

Avoid placing your burdens on others;
refrain from seeking dominance and
instead strive to serve.

10

There are many deceitful people;
be cautious about extending your hand to everyone.

Part 2

Ways to Increase Self-Esteem

11

What other desires can you have in the presence
of my affection?
When divinity is with you,
what more do you seek from humanity?

12

Do not focus on the yellowing leaves of the tree;
rather, harvest its apples, for they are ripe.
Do the yellow leaves lack meaning?
They signify maturity and wholeness.

13

I am enamoured by both His fury and His grace,
captivated by these contrasting qualities.

14

Pain is a valuable experience,
for it conceals numerous blessings within,
as the shell of a walnut
or almond encases its delicate and delicious core.

15

What constitutes the world?
A being oblivious to the divine,
not merely material possessions, wealth, power, or kinship.
The Prophet referred to wealth used
for faith as 'good wealth'.

16

A true pilgrim seeks fellowship with others on the journey,
regardless of whether they are Hindu, Turk, or Arab.
Do not focus on their appearance or skin colour;
instead, consider their resolve and intent.

17

One who is swayed by the slightest breeze is like straw,
for there are many adverse winds.
The gales of rage, lust, and greed –
these cause those lacking inner strength to bend.

18

What constitutes justice?
To assign each thing to its rightful place.
What constitutes oppression?
To displace things from their designated locations.

19

The discerning choose solitude,
for it purifies the heart.

20

No one shall bear another's burdens;
no one shall reap without first having sown.

Part 3

Problems of Lacking Self-Esteem

21

The loads carried by donkeys vary greatly;
do not drive them with a single stick.
One bears a load of rubies and gems,
another, sacks of stone and marble.

22

Why have you conflated the insignificant
with the meaningful?
Did you transfer oil from a glass?
People mocked his analogy,
he who thought himself fully clothed.

23

On spinning around and feeling dizzy,
it may seem as though the building is rotating,
but it is, in fact, you who are in motion.

24

Like the unsightly spider,
it weaves thick drapes
crafted from its own excretions.
It generates a luminous shroud from its own detritus,
obscuring its own discerning vision.

25

Each one befriended me based on their own assumptions;
they did not inquire into the mysteries I held.
My mind is close to my sorrow,
although my sight and hearing lack illumination.

26

From their different perspectives, their views diverged;
one referred to it as *dal*,
while another called it *alif*.[1]

---

1   Names of two Arabic letters of the alphabet.

27

As a being in the world,
you interpret it through your unique perspective;
you comprehend the whole
based on your individual character.

28

O humility, subjugated by fools;
O arrogance, subjugated by kings.
Such arrogance thrives among the vulgar.
Do not try to retreat, for its mirror reflects back on you.

29

The imitator is like an ill child,
despite having limited argumentation and reasoning.

30

The intoxication from wine is not unique;
all that is sensual obscures vision and hearing.
The devil did not drink wine;
he was made drunk by pride and laziness.

Part 4

Barriers
to Self-Esteem

31

When God wishes to unveil a person,
He guides them to criticize the virtuous.
When God intends to conceal an individual's flaws,
He encourages them to refrain
from discussing the deficiencies of the imperfect.

32

Harut[2] sprang from the celestial domain of the sky,
but owing to an admonition,
he became ensnared in that state.
He fell from favour by alienating himself from Truth,
positioning himself as the authority
and excluding others.

---

2   Harut and Marut are two fallen angels in Islamic belief.

33

The blind Pharaoh thought the sea was dry,
and so he advanced with might and power.
On entering, he was engulfed by a single droplet,
and his face was perpetually obscured.

34

The impoverished man, Adam,
failed to recognize his own identity,
as his rise in value caused him to feel smaller.

35

The most trivial of pleasures, in its grotesqueness, is jealousy; the same envy that caused Satan's demise.

36

The extent of injustice you perceive in others
is your own nature reflected in them!
You fail to recognize the evil within yourself;
else, you would become your own worst enemy.

37

O Pharaoh, do not be so arrogant;
you only possess cunning, not flamboyance.
Approaching the peacock will make
your display ineffective,
and leave you vulnerable.

38

The greedy vessel remained empty
until the clam revealed its hidden gem.

39

You wound yourself, O World;
your reflection resides within me.
You see your image in my form;
in your own struggle,
you have provoked yourself.

40

O fortunate one,
you who recognize your own imperfections.
Whoever points out a flaw takes responsibility for it.

Part 5
Ways to Enhance Self-Esteem

41

The essence of life comes solely from
experiences and challenges;
those with greater knowledge possess
a deeper understanding of existence.

42

You may understand the value of every commodity.
But if you are oblivious to your own worth,
you are a fool.

43

Without imperfections,
how could the value of gold be demonstrated?
Those who acknowledge and understand
their own deficiencies
move closer to their ideal state.

44

Aim to diminish your material and
worldly characteristics,
allowing your stone-like core to transform
into a shining diamond.

45

I serve the one who does not barter their existence,
except for the Sultan graced with the gifts of life.

46

According to the teachings of the saints,
both gentle and severe,
do not hide your body from Truth,
for your belief serves as your foundation.
The warmth and chill of life's seasons
embody the essence of sincerity and assurance in service.

47

The wise individual contemplates existence
and its elements,
reflecting on the destinies of
the Pharaohs and the people of 'Aad.[3]

---

3   An ancient Arabian tribe, mentioned in the Qur'an, destroyed by a storm
after rejecting monotheism.

48

In the absence of a standard measure,
neither creativity nor logic can be distinguished.
Quickly align both with a principle:
the Qur'an and the example of the prophets.
Every heart beckons: Come!

49

One must seek the sanctuary of God's grace,
for He bestows countless gifts upon souls.

50

I serve that illustrious person
who, aside from the Philosopher's Stone,
experiences no failure.

Part 6

The Role of Acceptance in Self-Actualization

51

Heal all the blind, except for the envious,
for the envious impose denial upon you.
Do not empower your envious nature,
even if it belongs to me,
for I will respond in kind.

52

Dissipate your fury; do not shatter the arrow;
your wrathful gaze measures the lion's blood.

53

They exhibited an insatiable desire for the unattainable; greed compels people to covet what is forbidden.

54

You are the one who inflicts wounds upon yourself;
in that instant, you condemn your own existence.

55

He said to the mirror:
'The man's unattractiveness is evident.'
It is the reflection that can solidify the appearance.
Your face must be like iron, resembling a mirror.
It says: 'Look at your own unappealing face.'

56

Expand your perception to the unadulterated
radiance of the sovereign.
And so, unlike the short-sighted,
you shall not be deceived into believing that this
encompasses everything,
merely grief and joy.
O Nothingness, why are you
devoid of inception or conclusion?

57

This barren location exists solely in your perception; the royal court is accessible to us.

58

Within us reside myriad wolves and swine,
both pure and evil,
virtuous and vile.
The dominant being governs all,
like the superiority of gold over copper
when both are shown side by side.

59

Patience resembles a golden bridge to Paradise.
Yet, with every virtue arises a harsh reality:
escaping the song results in disunion,
as the song is inseparable from the lover.

60

The wise do not fixate on profit or deficit,
for both, like a deluge, will swiftly dissolve.
Regardless of clarity or obscurity,
since it is transient,
do not allow it to be a source of worry.

Part 7

The Impact of Awareness on Self-Esteem

61

Those who are awake find themselves
in a deeper state of sleep;
their consciousness is overshadowed
by their unconsciousness.
As our spirits remain oblivious to Truth,
our perceived awareness is like a prison.

62

A person with an awakened heart,
though their physical eyes may be closed in sleep,
will perceive numerous inner visions.
If you have not yet embarked on this journey,
stay vigilant, pursue the essence,
and persist resolutely in your endeavour.

63

The animal soul is devoid of sleep,
yet an animal sleeps.
Its senses reflect the burdens of humanity.
On awakening, no animal remains sleeping;
its sensory perceptions stem
from the records of suffering.

64

The greater your alertness, the greater your suffering;
the deeper your awareness, the more pallid you appear.

65

The Prophet said:
'The breath of truth'
in current times establishes precedence.
Stay vigilant and acknowledge these moments;
embrace them with your hearts.

66

Awakening is enhanced by knowledge.
How profound it is to engage with the uninformed!

67

If you remain vigilant and alert,
you will observe the repercussions of your actions
at all times.

68

Many possess waking eyes but sleeping hearts.
What can those made only of water and clay
genuinely perceive?

69

Free yourself from this distraction;
elevate your consciousness from sleep to awareness.
Like the friends of the cave, O Lord,
awaken, lest you believe they have vanished.

70

My eyes are closed, yet my heart remains alert;
recognize my inactive state by my endeavours.
The Prophet said that the physical eyes do not sleep,
but the heart rests before the Lord of mankind.
Your eyes are open while your heart is asleep;
my eyes are closed, yet my heart is poised to awaken.

Part 8

The Impact
of Relationships
on Self-Actualization

71

My tears have transformed into an ocean
dedicated to the exquisite and the beloved.

72

The presents exchanged among friends
merely symbolize connection,
unless they reveal hidden passions beneath.

73

The celebration and assembly convey the reality
that we, esteemed guests,
have shared in this joy with you.
The presentations and tokens provided serve
as a testament to my satisfaction with you.

74

You are unique in my heart and soul,
blushing at your presence.
I frequently praised our people,
yet my true purpose was solely directed towards you
out of need.

75

I said:

'Your grievances are echoed by a cohort of parrots
just like you.'
A parrot sensed your anguish;
it ruptured its heart, collapsed, and died.

76

They are the lions among men in the world,
responding quickly when
the pleas of the oppressed resound.
On hearing the lamentations of the downtrodden,
they rush to their aid,
as though compelled by divine compassion.

77

That is the charity you extend to the grieving,
when you listen to their pleas.
You will hear the lamentations of the heartbroken,
the dignity of a noble spirit confined within a bodily form.

78

Although the lion may feel embarrassment among them,
he nonetheless honors and accompanies them.
And so the king arises from the army of compassion,
allying himself with the assembly of benevolence.
Similarly, the moon bears its own guilt,
yet it is celebrated for its kindness among the stars.

79

Exercise caution;
you should not feel shamed by the infamous.
Instead, remain vigilant with their secrets.

80

You must humble yourself to drink
the water of mercy
and, within, taste the wine of divine grace
and become inebriated.

Part 9

Obstacles to Creative Thinking

81

Obsolete perceptions of the narrow-minded
instill detrimental and erroneous notions
in the minds of others.

82

The aim is to forge a pathway
in the way a king should arise.

83

Distinctions arise from the True One,
as transformations emanate from Him.
The Truth affirms this to those who are
vigilant and perceptive.

84

Many people emerge from a society of imitation,
projecting upon themselves fragmented illusions.
They assert that their imitation
and reasoning form the foundation,
binding their wings and limiting their potential.

85

To attain clarity,
remove the veils of greed from your sight,
for the counterfeit Sufi, driven by greed,
has deprived his intellect of light and brilliance.

86

If the subconscious mind resembles tangled hair,
it should not seek the path of enlightenment.
If dormant ideas are few,
they yield only successive errors.

87

A significant danger awaits the imitator
emerging from the path:
the thief, and the devil.
But when they open their eyes and read the signs,
the devil within them releases its hold.

88

Those who harbour lofty ambitions and elevated thoughts
must recognize that such aspirations
stem from their own efforts.
A notion that does not arise from nature and intelligence
does not exist in the world;
if it does, it is merely your own thought.

89

Avoid seeking advancement through mere discourse;
for those who are patient,
listening brings greater rewards than speaking.

90

Observe the cauldrons of the mind simmering;
remain vigilant
and attentive even amidst the flames.

Part 10
Ways to Enhance Creativity

91

With each moment, an idea, like a cherished visitor,
enters your heart anew.
Embrace each thought as it arises,
welcoming it with joy and maximizing its potential.

92

O imitator, retreat from Bukhara!
Seek humility to become lion-hearted
in order to reveal another Bukhara within,
where the esteemed in the assembly
do not waste themselves.
Bukhara is a hub of diverse disciplines,
epitomizing secondary knowledge.

93

When affirmative thoughts and concepts engage a person,
pleasant reflections will enhance their intellect.

94

As long as you maintain constant awareness,
your thoughts will be guided by that awareness.
On becoming a confidant in the sanctuary of His Majesty,
you will undoubtedly perceive
the unblemished beauty of the Beloved.

95

The greater the number of intermediaries,
the more distant the union.
Yet, with fewer resources, the joy of connection intensifies.
When constrained by rationale, curiosity diminishes.
But it is curiosity that leads you to the essence of Truth.

96

Hearts refined through reflection and contemplation
allow the mirror of the soul
to retain its most pristine essence.
Eventually, through contemplation,
an opportunity will arise,
and your heart will affirm the authenticity
of your commitment.

97

Everyone deserves their aspirations,
and so we provide them with nourishment
for their passions.
To one, we offer love as sustenance;
to another, their spirit is guided by the Divine.
If joy and kindness are inherent to your nature,
why oppose the goodness that life offers?

98

If internal beliefs lack coherence and structure,
how can external behaviour be transformed?

99

The initial reflection, merely an imitation
through repetition, cultivates authenticity.
Until it is verified and becomes your personal narrative,
stay close to the pearl's shell,
allowing knowledge to flow.

100

Truth is only discovered through contrasts;
pain reveals the comforting resonance.

Finis